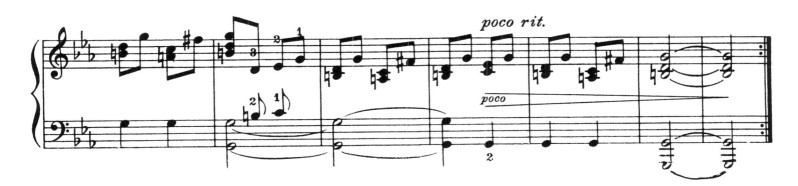

4

(1) Pedals in parenthesis are for the first time.
Pédales entre parenthèses sont pour la première fois.

PESCETTI

SONATA IN C MINOR

(transcribed by Carlos Salzedo)

for the harp

G. SCHIRMER, Inc.

DISTRIBUTED BY

HAL•LEONARD®
CORPORATION
7777 W. BLUEMOUND RD. P.O. BOX 13819 MILWAUKEE, WI 53213

Sonata
in C minor

Transcribed for Harp by
Carlos Salzedo
(1931)

Giovanni Battista Pescetti
1704-1766

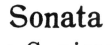

(1) Indications in parenthesis are for the repetition.
Indications entre parenthèses sont pour la reprise.

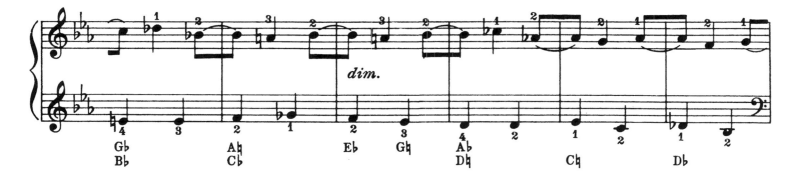

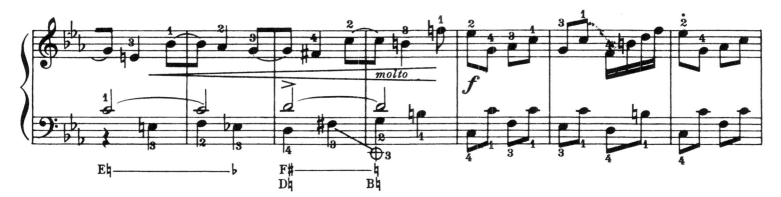

1ª volta, poco rall. e dim.
2ª volta, molto rall., ma senza dim.

Andantino espressivo

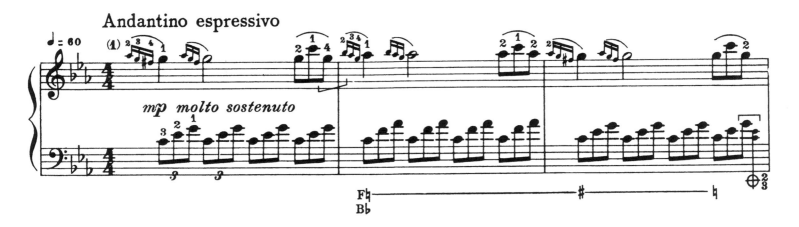

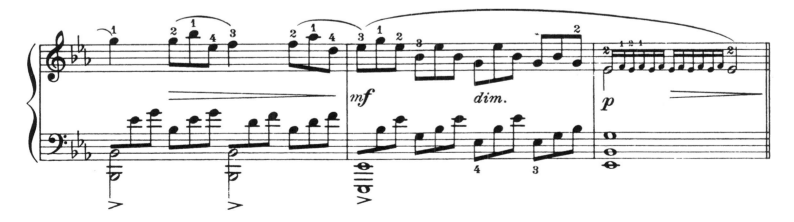

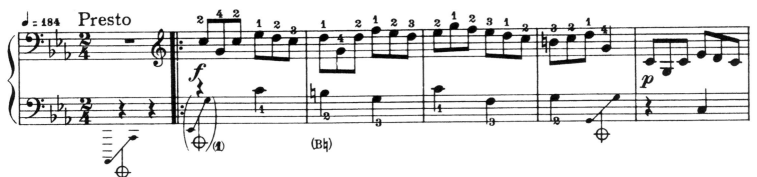

(1) Indications in parenthesis are for the repetition.
Indications entre parenthèses sont pour la reprise.

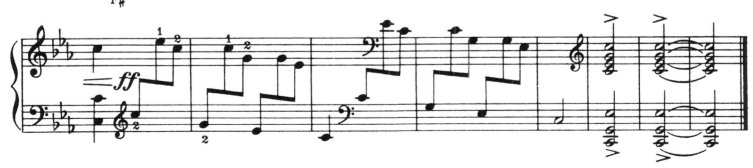

U.S. $7.99

HL50280450

ISBN-13: 978-0-7935-5566-6

Distributed By

HAL LEONARD

50280450